Practical Guide to OOP

Practical Guide

A. De Quattro

Copyright © 2024

Practical Guide

1. Introduction

Introduction to Object-Oriented Programming (OOP)

Object-Oriented Programming (OOP) is a programming paradigm that has revolutionized the way developers conceive and write software. It is based on the idea of modeling real-world problems using concepts such as objects, classes, inheritance, polymorphism, and encapsulation, thus offering a more intuitive and modular structure for writing code. This introduction will explore in detail what OOP is, its history and evolution, and the advantages it offers compared to other programming paradigms.

What is Object-Oriented Programming

Object-Oriented Programming (OOP) is a programming paradigm that is based on the concept of "objects" which can contain data, in the form of attributes, and code, in the form of methods. Objects are instances of "classes," which serve as blueprints or models for creating objects with similar characteristics. This paradigm is distinguished by its ability to model and organize software in a way that reflects the reality of the world it aims to represent.

Fundamental Concepts of OOP

1. **Class**: A class is a construct that defines a type of object. It specifies the data (attributes) and behaviors (methods) that objects created from it will have. For example, a class `Car` might have attributes such as `color`, `model`, and `year`, and methods like `accelerate()` and `brake()`.

2. **Object**: An object is an instance of a class. If the class `Car` is the blueprint, a specific `2020 red Car` is the object. Objects are concrete entities that exist in memory and interact with each other through methods

defined in their classes.

3. **Encapsulation**: Encapsulation is the property that allows hiding the internal details of an object, exposing only what is necessary for the object's use. In practice, an object's attributes are often made private and accessible only through public methods called getters and setters.

4. **Inheritance**: Inheritance is the mechanism by which a class can inherit attributes and methods from another class, called a base class or superclass. This allows code reuse and the creation of class hierarchies. For example, you might have a class `Vehicle` with common attributes and methods, and derived classes like `Car` and `Motorcycle` that inherit from `Vehicle` but add specific features.

5. **Polymorphism**: Polymorphism allows objects to be treated as instances of their superclass but behave differently based on

their concrete class. This means a method can be implemented differently in different classes while keeping the same name. For example, a method `calculateArea()` might be implemented differently in the `Circle` and `Square` classes but can be called in the same way on an instance of either class.

6. **Abstraction**: Abstraction allows defining interfaces or abstract classes that outline a contract for derived classes. These derived classes must implement the methods defined in the interface or abstract class, but the details of the implementation are hidden.

These fundamental concepts enable developers to build complex software in a more organized and maintainable way, making it easier to manage and evolve code over time.

History and Evolution of OOP

OOP did not emerge suddenly but is the result of a long evolution of thought on programming. Its history begins in the 1960s and has gone through several phases of development before becoming one of the most widespread and appreciated programming paradigms.

The Roots in the 1960s

The origin of OOP dates back to the 1960s when Ole-Johan Dahl and Kristen Nygaard from the Norwegian Computing Center in Oslo began developing the Simula programming language. Simula, initially designed to simulate real systems, is considered the first object-oriented programming language. It introduced fundamental concepts like classes and objects, which allowed modeling real-world entities in a natural way.

Simula was revolutionary in its approach to programming, as it allowed developers to create objects that represented real-world concepts, with their own states and behaviors. This innovation marked the starting point for the development of other object-oriented languages.

The Emergence of OOP in the 1970s and 1980s

In the 1970s, the idea of OOP continued to develop, influencing various programming languages. One key moment was the creation of Smalltalk by Alan Kay and his team at Xerox PARC in the early 1970s. Smalltalk was the first language to be entirely object-oriented, and its development environment introduced many concepts that are now taken for granted, such as the graphical user interface (GUI) and interactive development.

Smalltalk had a huge impact on the computing community and inspired many of the subsequent programming languages, including Objective-C, C++, and Java. In particular,

Smalltalk demonstrated how OOP could be used not only for simulations but also for building entire software systems.

C++ is another key language in the evolution of OOP, developed by Bjarne Stroustrup in the early 1980s as an extension of the C language. C++ combined the efficiency and flexibility of C with OOP concepts, making it a powerful tool for developing complex software. C++ introduced the concept of multiple inheritance and refined encapsulation and polymorphism, making it one of the most widely used languages for system software, games, and enterprise software development.

The Spread of OOP in the 1990s

In the 1990s, OOP became the dominant methodology for software development, largely due to the widespread adoption of Java. Java, developed by Sun Microsystems and released in 1995, was designed from the ground up to be an object-oriented, portable, and secure language. Its "write once, run anywhere" philosophy made it extremely popular for web and mobile application development.

Java consolidated many OOP concepts and made them accessible to a wide range of developers. Its simple syntax, automatic memory management (via garbage collection), and strong type system helped spread OOP on a large scale, leading many developers to consider it the default programming paradigm.

During this period, OOP was also adopted in other languages such as Python, Ruby, and Objective-C, further expanding its use. Each of these languages brought its own interpretation of OOP but shared the fundamental concepts of classes, objects, and encapsulation.

OOP in the 21st Century

In the 21st century, OOP has continued to evolve, with languages like C# from Microsoft and Swift from Apple introducing new ideas and improvements to the paradigm. C# was introduced as part of Microsoft's .NET platform and combines features of C++ and Java with new functionalities like LINQ and asynchronous multitasking. Swift, on the other hand, was developed by Apple as a safer and more user-friendly language compared to Objective-C and has quickly gained popularity among iOS and macOS application developers.

Today, OOP is the dominant programming paradigm, used in a wide range of applications from operating systems to games, from enterprise software to mobile apps. However, it is important to note that OOP is not the only existing paradigm; other paradigms, such as functional programming, are gaining ground, and many developers combine techniques from different paradigms to achieve the best results.

Advantages of Object-Oriented Programming

OOP offers numerous advantages over other programming paradigms, making it particularly suited for developing complex and large-scale software. Below are some of the main advantages of OOP.

1. **Modularity**

One of the main advantages of OOP is its ability to break down a complex program into smaller, more manageable modules. Each module can be represented as a class or a group of classes, each with a well-defined responsibility. This approach makes it easier to write, understand, and maintain code, as developers can focus on individual parts of the system without needing to grasp the entire codebase.

Modularity also facilitates code reuse, as

classes can be reused in different projects or parts of the system. This reduces code duplication and decreases the risk of errors, improving the overall quality of the software.

2. **Maintainability**

Encapsulation, one of the pillars of OOP, enhances software maintainability. By hiding the internal details of objects and exposing only well-defined public interfaces, OOP allows modifications to be made to the code without affecting other parts of the system. This is particularly important in large projects where changes can have disruptive effects if not properly isolated.

Inheritance and polymorphism further contribute to maintainability by allowing developers to extend the behavior of software without modifying existing code. For example, new features can be added by creating new classes that inherit from existing ones, reducing the need to rewrite code.

3. **Reusability**

One of the main goals of OOP is to promote code reuse. Classes and objects can be easily reused in different contexts due to their modular and independent nature. Inheritance allows for the creation of new classes based on existing ones, reusing the code that has already been written and reducing the amount of new code that needs to be developed from scratch.

Moreover, many object-oriented libraries and frameworks provide a wide range of predefined classes and objects that can be used as a foundation for building complex applications. This speeds up development and allows developers to focus on the unique aspects of their application rather than reinventing common functionality.

4. **Flexibility and Extensibility**

OOP offers a high degree of flexibility and extensibility. Developers can extend software functionality without having to rewrite existing code. This is possible due to inheritance, which allows creating new classes based on existing ones, and polymorphism, which allows treating objects generically regardless of their specific class.

Additionally, OOP facilitates the adoption of new requirements and the addition of new features, as classes can be extended or modified without affecting the rest of the system. This flexibility is particularly valuable in agile development environments where requirements can change rapidly and frequently.

5. **Better Modeling of Real-World Problems**

One of the most significant advantages of OOP is its ability to model complex real-world problems in an intuitive manner. Objects, with their states and behaviors, directly reflect real-world entities, making software design and understanding easier. This makes OOP particularly useful for creating simulations, games, and applications that interact with real-world data and processes.

6. **Reliability and Robustness**

Encapsulation and inheritance contribute to creating more reliable and robust software. Encapsulation prevents users from directly manipulating the internal states of objects, reducing the risk of errors. Inheritance and polymorphism allow extending class behaviors in a controlled and predictable manner, improving system stability.

Moreover, OOP facilitates the implementation of unit and integration testing, as classes can be tested in isolation, ensuring that each part of the system functions correctly before being integrated with other parts.

7. **Managing Complexity**

OOP helps manage software complexity, especially in large-scale projects. By breaking down the system into objects and classes, developers can tackle complex problems incrementally, focusing on one part at a time. This approach reduces cognitive complexity and facilitates team collaboration, as each team member can work on separate parts of the system.

8. **Adaptability to Changes**

OOP allows for easy adaptation to changing requirements. Since software is divided into independent modules, changes to one part of the system do not necessarily require changes to other parts. This makes updating software and evolving it over time simpler, keeping the system flexible and responsive to new needs.

9. **Support for Frameworks and Design Patterns**

OOP is strongly supported by a wide range of frameworks and design patterns that facilitate the development of complex applications. Design patterns, such as Singleton, Factory Method, Observer, and many others, are reusable solutions to common software design problems and are based on OOP principles. Using these patterns allows for writing more efficient, readable, and maintainable code, reducing the risk of errors and improving overall software quality.

Additionally, many modern frameworks, such as Spring for Java, Django for Python, and Ruby on Rails for Ruby, are built around OOP concepts, providing powerful tools for managing dependencies, inversion of control, and component-based architecture.

10. **Collaboration and Team Development**

Finally, OOP facilitates collaboration and team development. Since code is organized into classes and modules, different team members can work on different parts of the project in parallel, reducing conflicts and improving efficiency. Furthermore, the use of well-defined interfaces and encapsulation ensures that team members can develop software independently without worrying about the internal details of classes developed by others.

Object-Oriented Programming represents one of the most important and widespread programming paradigms in computer science history. Its ability to model the real world through concepts like objects, classes, inheritance, and polymorphism has made software development more intuitive, modular, and maintainable. Through its history, from the 1960s with Simula and

Smalltalk, to languages like C++, Java, Python, and Swift, OOP has demonstrated its flexibility and power, becoming the paradigm of choice for developing complex and large-scale applications.

The advantages of OOP, including modularity, maintainability, reusability, and robustness, make it an ideal choice for most software projects. Although other programming paradigms exist, OOP continues to be relevant and evolving, adapting to new needs and technologies, and remaining a fundamental reference for every developer.

2. Fundamental Concepts of OOP

Object-Oriented Programming (OOP) is a programming paradigm that organizes code into distinct blocks called objects, which are representations of real-world or conceptual entities. This approach facilitates the design, maintenance, and expansion of complex software. To fully grasp OOP, it is essential to familiarize yourself with the fundamental concepts that form its structure. In this detailed discussion, we will explore the concepts of classes and objects, attributes and methods, and constructors and destructors, providing a solid foundation for anyone wishing to delve deeper into OOP.

Classes and Objects

The concept of classes and objects is at the heart of Object-Oriented Programming. A class represents a model, a sort of blueprint, for creating objects, which are concrete instances of that class. This section will explore the definition of a class and the process of creating objects.

Definition of a Class

A **class** can be seen as a model or schema from which objects are created. It defines the properties (attributes) and behaviors (methods) that the objects created from it will have. Simply put, a class is a collection of variables and functions grouped under a single name. The variables contained within a class are called **attributes** (or fields), while the functions are called **methods**.

Syntax of a Class

In many programming languages, such as Python, Java, C++, a class is defined using the `class` keyword followed by the class name. Here is an example in Python:

```python
class Car:
    make = "Toyota"
    model = "Corolla"
    year = 2020

    def start_engine(self):
        print("Engine started")
```

In this example, `Car` is the class name. The `Car` class has three attributes (`make`, `model`, and `year`) and one method (`start_engine`). The attributes represent the object's state, while the method represents the object's behavior.

Visibility and Access Modifiers

In many OOP languages, the attributes and

methods of a class can have access modifiers that determine their visibility with respect to other classes. The most common are:

- **Public**: Attributes and methods declared as `public` are accessible from any part of the program.

- **Private**: Attributes and methods declared as `private` are accessible only within the class in which they are defined.

- **Protected**: Attributes and methods declared as `protected` are accessible within the class in which they are defined and in derived classes (subclasses).

For example, in C++, the definition of a class with access modifiers might look like this:

```cpp
class Car {
private:
```

```cpp
    std::string make;
    std::string model;
    int year;

public:
    Car(std::string m, std::string mo, int y) : make(m), model(mo), year(y) {}

    void startEngine() {
        std::cout << "Engine started" << std::endl;
    }
};
```

In this example, the attributes `make`, `model`, and `year` are private, so they are not accessible directly from outside the class. The method `startEngine` is public, so it can be called on a `Car` object created outside the class.

Creating Objects

Objects are concrete instances of classes. When you create an object, you are essentially creating a specific instance of a class, complete with its own attributes and methods. Creating an object involves calling a **constructor**, a special function that initializes the object.

Creating Objects in Practice

Continuing with the example of the `Car` class in Python, an object is created as follows:

```python
my_car = Car()
```

In this case, `my_car` is an object of the `Car` class. Once the object is created, you can access its attributes and methods as follows:

```python
print(my_car.make)  # Output: Toyota
my_car.start_engine()  # Output: Engine started
```

In Python, the `my_car` object has access to all the attributes and methods defined in the `Car` class.

Multiple Objects

One of the main advantages of OOP is the ability to create multiple objects from the same class. Each object will be independent of the others, but all share the same basic structure. For example, you might create several `Car` objects:

```python
car1 = Car()
car2 = Car()
```

Both objects, `car1` and `car2`, are instances of the `Car` class, but they can have different internal states (attribute values) depending on how they are manipulated.

Object State and Differences Between Instance and Class

One of the critical aspects of OOP is understanding the difference between the **class** and the **instance** (object) of the class. The class defines the structure and behavior, but does not maintain state; the state is held in the individual instances. Each instance has its own copy of the data (attributes) defined in the class.

For example, if `car1` and `car2` are both objects of the `Car` class, they can have different states:

```python
car1.make = "Honda"
car2.make = "Ford"

print(car1.make)  # Output: Honda
print(car2.make)  # Output: Ford
```

Even though `car1` and `car2` are based on the same `Car` class, their states (in this case, the value of the `make` attribute) can differ.

Attributes and Methods

Attributes and methods are the fundamental components of a class. Attributes represent the data that an object can contain, while methods represent the operations an object can perform. Understanding these concepts is essential to fully harness the power of Object-Oriented Programming.

Class Attributes

Class attributes are variables that belong to a class and are shared by all instances of that class. There are two main types of attributes:

1. **Instance Attributes**: These are attributes specific to each object created from a class. Each object will have its own copy of these attributes. Instance attributes are typically defined within the constructor of the class.

2. **Class Attributes**: These attributes are shared among all instances of a class. This means that if the class attribute is changed, the change is visible in all instances of the class. Class attributes are defined directly in the class, outside of any method.

Instance Attributes

Instance attributes are defined within a special method called a **constructor**. In Python, the constructor is the `__init__()` method. Here's an example:

```python
class Car:
    def __init__(self, make, model, year):
        self.make = make
        self.model = model
        self.year = year
```

```

In this case, `make`, `model`, and `year` are instance attributes. Each time a new `Car` object is created, these attributes are set with the values provided during the creation of the object.

```python
car1 = Car("Toyota", "Corolla", 2020)
car2 = Car("Honda", "Civic", 2021)

print(car1.make)  # Output: Toyota
print(car2.make)  # Output: Honda
```

As you can see, each `Car` object has its own copy of the `make`, `model`, and `year` attributes, independent of the others.
```

Class Attributes

Class attributes are shared among all instances of a class. They are defined directly in the class and not within any method. Here's an example in Python:

```python
class Car:
    number_of_wheels = 4  # Class attribute

    def __init__(self, make, model, year):
        self.make = make
        self.model = model
        self.year = year
```

In this case, `number_of_wheels` is a class attribute. Since it is shared by all instances of the `Car` class, if it is modified, the change is visible in all instances:

```python
car1 = Car("Toyota", "Corolla", 2020)
car2 = Car("Honda", "Civic", 2021)

print(car1.number_of_wheels)  # Output: 4
print(car2.number_of_wheels)  # Output: 4

Car.number_of_wheels = 5  # Modify the class attribute

print(car1.number_of_wheels)  # Output: 5
print(car2.number_of_wheels)  # Output: 5
```

In this example, the modification of the class attribute `number_of_wheels` is visible in all instances of `Car`.

Class Methods

Methods are functions defined within a class and are used to manipulate the attributes of an object or to perform other operations related to the object. Methods can be divided into different categories, including instance methods, class methods, and static methods.

Instance Methods

Instance methods operate on individual instances of a class. These methods can access and modify instance attributes, and can also call other methods of the same class. To define an instance method, you need to include `self` as the first parameter of the method. `self` represents the current instance of the class.

Here's an example:

```python
class Car:
    def __init__(self, make, model, year):
        self.make = make
        self.model = model
        self.year = year

    def start_engine(self):
        print(f"The engine of the {self.make} {self.model} is started.")
```

In this case, `start_engine` is an instance method. It can be called on a `Car` object to perform a specific action related to that object:

```python
car1 = Car("Toyota", "Corolla", 2020)
```

car1.start_engine() # Output: The engine of the Toyota Corolla is started.

```

#### Class Methods

Class methods operate on the class itself, rather than on individual instances. They are often used to define methods that are related to the class as a whole, rather than to any specific instance. In Python, class methods are defined using the `@classmethod` decorator, and they take `cls` (the class itself) as their first parameter.

Here's an example:

```python
class Car:

```
    number_of_wheels = 4 # Class attribute

    def __init__(self, make, model, year):
        self.make = make
        self.model = model
        self.year = year

    @classmethod
    def change_number_of_wheels(cls, new_number):
        cls.number_of_wheels = new_number
```

In this example, `change_number_of_wheels` is a class method that modifies the class attribute `number_of_wheels`. It can be called directly on the class:

```python
```

```
Car.change_number_of_wheels(6)
print(Car.number_of_wheels)  # Output: 6
```

Static Methods

Static methods are methods that do not operate on an instance or the class itself. They are defined using the `@staticmethod` decorator and do not take `self` or `cls` as a parameter. Static methods are often used to perform operations that are related to the class, but that do not require access to the class or instance attributes.

Here's an example:

```python
class Car:
    @staticmethod
```

```
def display_message():
    print("This is a static method.")
```

In this case, `display_message` is a static method and can be called directly on the class:

```python
Car.display_message()  # Output: This is a static method.
```

Static methods are useful for utility functions that do not need to access the class or instance attributes but are still related to the class's overall purpose.

Constructors and Destructors

Constructors and **destructors** are

special methods that are used to manage the creation and destruction of objects. The constructor initializes a new object, setting its initial state, while the destructor cleans up resources when the object is no longer needed.

Constructors

The constructor is a special method that is automatically called when a new object is created. It is responsible for initializing the object's attributes and setting up any necessary state. In Python, the constructor is defined by the `__init__` method, while in languages like C++ or Java, it has the same name as the class.

Here is an example in Python:

```python
class Car:
    def __init__(self, make, model, year):
```

```
        self.make = make
        self.model = model
        self.year = year

car1 = Car("Toyota", "Corolla", 2020)
```

In this example, the `__init__` method is the constructor that initializes the attributes `make`, `model`, and `year` for the `Car` object.

Overloading Constructors

In some programming languages, such as C++, constructors can be overloaded, meaning that you can define multiple constructors with different parameters. Python does not support constructor overloading directly, but you can achieve similar functionality by using default arguments or by using class methods.

Here is an example in C++:

```cpp
class Car {
public:
    std::string make;
    std::string model;
    int year;

    Car(std::string m, std::string mo, int y) : make(m), model(mo), year(y) {}

    Car(std::string m, std::string mo) : make(m), model(mo), year(0) {}
};

Car car1("Toyota", "Corolla", 2020);
Car car2("Honda", "Civic");
```

```

In this case, the `Car` class has two constructors: one that takes three arguments and another that takes two arguments.

### Destructors

The destructor is a special method that is called when an object is destroyed or goes out of scope. It is used to clean up any resources that the object may have acquired during its lifetime, such as memory or file handles. In Python, the destructor is defined by the `__del__` method, while in C++ it is defined by a method with the same name as the class but preceded by a tilde (`~`).

Here is an example in Python:

```python

```python
class Car:
    def __init__(self, make, model, year):
        self.make = make
        self.model = model
        self.year = year

    def __del__(self):
        print(f"The {self.make} {self.model} has been destroyed.")
```

In this case, the `__del__` method is the destructor, which is called automatically when the `Car` object is destroyed.

In C++, the destructor might look like this:

```cpp
class Car {
```

```cpp
public:
    ~Car() {
        std::cout << "Car destroyed" << std::endl;
    }
};
```

In this example, the destructor is called automatically when the `Car` object goes out of scope or is explicitly deleted.

When Are Constructors and Destructors Called?

- **Constructors** are called automatically when a new object is created. They are used to set up the initial state of the object and perform any necessary initialization tasks.

- **Destructors** are called automatically when an object is destroyed. They are used to release any resources that the object may have acquired and perform any necessary cleanup tasks.

In Python, destructors are called when the object is garbage-collected, which may not happen immediately after the object goes out of scope. In C++, destructors are called immediately when an object goes out of scope or is explicitly deleted.

Conclusion

Object-Oriented Programming (OOP) is a powerful paradigm that helps developers create modular, maintainable, and reusable code. By organizing code into classes and objects, OOP allows you to model real-world or conceptual entities, making complex systems easier to understand and work with.

The fundamental concepts of OOP, including classes and objects, attributes and methods, and constructors and destructors, provide the building blocks for creating sophisticated software systems. By mastering these concepts, you will be well-equipped to tackle the challenges of modern software development.

3. Fundamental Principles of OOP

Object-Oriented Programming (OOP) is a programming paradigm that relies on fundamental concepts that enable the structuring and organization of code in a more efficient and natural way, aligned with the real world. Among the core principles of OOP are **encapsulation**, **inheritance**, and **polymorphism**. These principles not only define how code is structured and organized but also how it interacts and evolves over time. Let's explore each of these concepts in detail, understanding their functionality, benefits, and practical implementations.

Encapsulation

Encapsulation is one of the most fundamental principles of OOP, referring to the practice of limiting access to an object's internal details, exposing only what is necessary for external use. This principle improves code security, integrity, and modularity.

Access Modifiers

Access modifiers are tools used to control the visibility level of a class's attributes and methods. There are several access modifiers, and the choice depends on the level of protection desired for class members.

Public Modifier (`public`)

A class member declared `public` is accessible from any other class. This means that there is no restriction on access, and `public` members can be freely used by other objects. However, excessive use of the `public` modifier can compromise the integrity of the code, as it allows any part of the program to directly modify the object's state.

```cpp
class Car {
```

```cpp
public:
    std::string brand;
    void startEngine() {
        std::cout << "Engine started." << std::endl;
    }
};
```

In this C++ example, both the `brand` attribute and the `startEngine` method are `public`, so they are accessible from any other class.

Private Modifier (`private`)

A class member declared `private` is accessible only within the same class. This modifier is used to protect data and ensure that it cannot be directly modified or used by other classes. It is a key tool for implementing encapsulation, as it allows hiding implementation details and exposing only the public interface of the class.

```cpp
class Car {
private:
    std::string brand;
    void startEngine() {
        std::cout << "Engine started." << std::endl;
    }
};
```

In this example, `brand` and `startEngine` are `private`, so they are not accessible outside the `Car` class.

Protected Modifier (`protected`)

A class member declared `protected` is similar to `private`, except that it is also accessible by derived classes (subclasses). This modifier is useful when you want to hide the internal details of the class but allow child classes to access these members to extend functionality.

```cpp
class Car {
protected:
    std::string brand;
    void startEngine() {
        std::cout << "Engine started." << std::endl;
    }
};
```

In this case, a subclass of `Car` can access the `brand` attribute and the `startEngine` method, but these members remain inaccessible outside the class hierarchy.

Getters and Setters

To allow controlled access to a class's private attributes, **getters** and **setters** are often used. These are public methods that provide an interface for reading or modifying private attributes while maintaining control over how and when such changes can be made.

Getter

A **getter** is a method that returns the value of a private attribute. It is used to access attributes in a controlled way without directly exposing the attribute.

```cpp
class Car {
private:
```

```
    std::string brand;

public:

    std::string getBrand() const {

        return brand;

    }
};
```

In this example, `getBrand` is a getter that returns the value of the `brand` attribute. Being a public method, it allows access to the value without directly exposing the attribute.

Setter

A **setter** is a method that allows modifying the value of a private attribute. It enables adding control or validation logic before accepting a new value for the attribute.

```cpp
class Car {
private:
    std::string brand;

public:
    void setBrand(const std::string& newBrand) {
        if (!newBrand.empty()) {
            brand = newBrand;
        }
    }
};
```

In this example, `setBrand` is a setter that sets the value of `brand`. The setter checks that the new value is not an empty string before assigning it, thus ensuring data integrity.

Benefits of Encapsulation

Encapsulation offers numerous advantages:

- **Data Protection**: Private attributes cannot be directly modified from outside the class, reducing the risk of errors and maintaining data integrity.

- **Modularity**: By hiding implementation details, encapsulation allows for internal modifications of a class without affecting the rest of the code. This facilitates software maintenance and expansion.

- **Access Control**: Getters and setters enable control over how attributes are read or modified, allowing validation or data transformation logic to be added.

- **Reduced Complexity**: Exposing only a public interface simplifies the use of the class by other parts of the program, as there is no need to understand internal details to use it correctly.

Inheritance

Inheritance is another fundamental principle of OOP and represents the ability of a class to inherit attributes and methods from another class. This allows for the creation of a class hierarchy that shares common functionalities, reducing code duplication and facilitating the extension of functionalities.

Concept of Inheritance

Inheritance allows the definition of a new class (called a **derived class** or **subclass**) based on an existing class (called a **base class** or **superclass**). The derived class inherits all the attributes and methods of the base class but can also add new attributes and methods or modify existing ones.

Example of Inheritance

Let's consider an example where we have a `Vehicle` class, representing a generic vehicle, and a `Car` class representing a specific car:

```cpp
class Vehicle {
public:
   int speed;

   void accelerate() {
     speed += 10;
   }
};


class Car : public Vehicle {
public:
   int numberOfDoors;
```

```
    void openDoor() {
        std::cout << "Door opened." << std::endl;
    }
};
```

In this example, the `Car` class inherits the `speed` attribute and the `accelerate` method from the `Vehicle` class. Additionally, the `Car` class adds a new attribute `numberOfDoors` and a method `openDoor`.

```cpp
Car myCar;

myCar.accelerate(); // Uses the method inherited from Vehicle

myCar.openDoor(); // Uses the method defined in Car
```

Single and Multiple Inheritance

Inheritance can be of two types: **single** and **multiple**.

Single Inheritance

Single inheritance occurs when a class derives from a single superclass. This is the most common type of inheritance and is supported by most OOP languages, such as Java and C#.

```java
class Vehicle {
    // Attributes and methods
}

class Car extends Vehicle {
```

    // Additional attributes and methods
}
```

In this Java example, the `Car` class extends `Vehicle`, inheriting its attributes and methods.

#### Multiple Inheritance

**Multiple inheritance** occurs when a class derives from more than one superclass. This type of inheritance is supported by some languages like C++, but it is not present in others, like Java, due to the complexity it introduces.

```cpp
class Engine {
public:

```cpp
    void startEngine() {
        std::cout << "Engine started." << std::endl;
    }
};


class Bodywork {
public:
    void openDoor() {
        std::cout << "Door opened." << std::endl;
    }
};


class Car : public Engine, public Bodywork {
    // Car inherits from both Engine and Bodywork
};
```

In this C++ example, `Car` inherits from both the `Engine` and `Bodywork` classes, gaining access to the methods of both.

Method Override and Overload

When using inheritance, it may be necessary to modify or extend the behavior of inherited methods. This is achieved through **method overriding** and **method overloading**.

Method Override

Method overriding allows providing a new implementation for a method inherited from a superclass. This enables the customization of the method's behavior in the subclass.

```cpp
class Vehicle {
```

```cpp
public:
    virtual void accelerate() {
        std::cout << "The vehicle accelerates." << std::endl;
    }
};


class Car : public Vehicle {
public:
    void accelerate() override {  // Method override
        std::cout << "The car accelerates quickly." << std::endl;
    }
};
```

In this C++ example, the `Car` class overrides the `accelerate` method from `Vehicle` to provide a version specific to `Car`.

Method Overload

Method overloading allows defining multiple versions of a method with the same name but with different parameters. This enables handling different situations with a single interface.

```cpp
class Math {
public:
    int sum(int a, int b) {
        return a + b;
    }

    double sum(double a, double b) {
        return a + b;
    }
};
```

```

In this example, the `Math` class has two `sum` methods, one that accepts integers and one that accepts floating-point numbers. The compiler determines which method to call based on the types of the arguments passed.

## Polymorphism

**Polymorphism** is a key principle of OOP that allows treating objects of different classes as if they were of the same type, thanks to their inheritance relationship. This principle enables writing more flexible and reusable code.

### Definition of Polymorphism

The term polymorphism comes from the Greek "poly" (many) and "morphé" (forms), indicating the ability to take on different
```

forms. In OOP, polymorphism allows a method to behave differently depending on the object calling it, even if the method has the same name across different classes.

Types of Polymorphism

There are two main types of polymorphism: **compile-time polymorphism** and **runtime polymorphism**.

Compile-time Polymorphism (Method Overloading)

Compile-time polymorphism is achieved through method overloading, where the decision on which method to call is made during the compilation of the program, based on the method's signature.

```cpp
class Math {
public:
    int sum(int a, int b) {
        return a + b;
    }

    double sum(double a, double b) {
        return a + b;
    }
};
```

As seen earlier, in this case, the compiler decides which version of the `sum` method to use based on the types of the parameters.

Runtime Polymorphism (Method Overriding)

Runtime polymorphism is achieved through method overriding and occurs when the method to be executed is determined at runtime, depending on the type of the object. This type of polymorphism is crucial for implementing more flexible and reusable code, especially when using inheritance.

```cpp
class Vehicle {
public:
    virtual void accelerate() {
        std::cout << "The vehicle accelerates." << std::endl;
    }
};


class Car : public Vehicle {
public:
    void accelerate() override {
```

```cpp
        std::cout << "The car accelerates quickly." << std::endl;
    }
};

void testDrive(Vehicle* v) {
    v->accelerate();
}
```

In this C++ example, the `testDrive` function accepts a pointer to a `Vehicle` object, but when a `Car` object is passed, the overridden `accelerate` method of `Car` is called, demonstrating runtime polymorphism.

Benefits of Polymorphism

Polymorphism offers several advantages in software development:

- **Code Flexibility**: Polymorphism allows writing code that can work with objects of different types in a unified way, without needing to know the specific type at compile time.

- **Code Reusability**: With polymorphism, functions and methods can operate on objects of different types, reducing code duplication and facilitating reuse.

- **Maintainability**: By using polymorphism, code can be extended or modified without altering existing code, making maintenance easier.

Object-Oriented Programming's fundamental principles—**encapsulation**, **inheritance**, and **polymorphism**—provide a robust foundation for structuring, organizing, and extending code. These principles help create modular, flexible, and reusable systems, reducing complexity and improving maintainability. Encapsulation protects data and controls access, inheritance promotes code reuse and hierarchies, and polymorphism enables flexibility and dynamic behavior in programs. Mastery of these concepts is essential for effective OOP and for building sophisticated and scalable software solutions.

4. Design and Architecture in Object-Oriented Programming (OOP)

Software design and architecture are fundamental aspects of developing robust, maintainable, and scalable applications. Specifically, in the context of Object-Oriented Programming (OOP), these aspects focus on code organization, adherence to specific principles, and the use of established design patterns. This discussion explores in detail the **design principles** of OOP, including the **SOLID**, **DRY**, and **KISS** principles, and delves into **design patterns** with particular attention to common patterns like **Singleton**, **Factory**, **Observer**, and **Strategy**.

OOP Design Principles

Design principles are guidelines that help developers design well-structured and flexible software systems. Adhering to these principles contributes to creating code that is not only functional but also easy to maintain and modify over time.

SOLID Principles

The SOLID principles are five object-oriented design principles introduced by Robert C. Martin, aiming to improve code maintainability and flexibility.

Single Responsibility Principle (SRP)

The **Single Responsibility Principle** states that a class should have one, and only one, reason to change. In other words, a class should have a single responsibility or purpose. This principle reduces complexity and facilitates code maintenance since each class is dedicated to a specific task.

Example:

Suppose we have an `Order` class that handles both the order processing logic and its persistence in the database. According to SRP, these two responsibilities should be separated into two classes: an `OrderProcessing` class to handle the order logic and a `DatabaseManagement` class to handle persistence.

```java
class OrderProcessing {
    public void process(Order order) {
        // Order processing logic
    }
}


class DatabaseManagement {
    public void save(Order order) {
        // Database saving logic
    }
```

```
}
```

Open/Closed Principle (OCP)

The **Open/Closed Principle** states that a class should be open for extension but closed for modification. This means that the behavior of a class should be extendable without modifying its existing code, usually through inheritance or interface implementation.

Example:

Consider a `Payment` class that calculates payment based on different modes (cash, credit card). Instead of modifying the class every time a new payment mode is added, we can use the OCP principle:

```java
```

```java
interface PaymentMethod {
    void pay(double amount);
}


class CashPayment implements PaymentMethod {
    public void pay(double amount) {
        // Logic for cash payment
    }
}


class CreditCardPayment implements PaymentMethod {
    public void pay(double amount) {
        // Logic for credit card payment
    }
}
```

New payment methods can be added by

implementing the `PaymentMethod` interface, without modifying the existing class.

Liskov Substitution Principle (LSP)

The **Liskov Substitution Principle** states that instances of a subclass should be able to replace instances of the superclass without altering the program's correctness. This principle ensures that subclasses maintain the behavior expected by the superclass.

Example:

Suppose we have a `Vehicle` class and a subclass `Car`:

```java
class Vehicle {
    public void start() {
```

```
        System.out.println("The vehicle is started.");
    }
}

class Car extends Vehicle {
    public void start() {
        System.out.println("The car is started.");
    }
}
```

According to the LSP, an object of type `Car` should be usable in place of an object of type `Vehicle` without causing issues.

Interface Segregation Principle (ISP)

The **Interface Segregation Principle** states

that clients should not be forced to depend on interfaces they do not use. This principle promotes the creation of specific interfaces rather than generic interfaces that group too many unrelated functionalities.

Example:

Instead of having a `Machine` interface with unrelated methods:

```java
interface Machine {
    void start();
    void stop();
    void rechargeBattery();
    void changeOil();
}
```

We can break it down into more specific interfaces:

```java
interface Startable {
    void start();
    void stop();
}

interface ElectricalMaintenance {
    void rechargeBattery();
}

interface MechanicalMaintenance {
    void changeOil();
}
```

Now, an `ElectricCar` class can implement only the interfaces relevant to it.

Dependency Inversion Principle (DIP)

The **Dependency Inversion Principle** states that high-level modules should not depend on low-level modules, but both should depend on abstractions (interfaces or abstract classes). Furthermore, abstractions should not depend on details, but details should depend on abstractions.

Example:

Instead of having an `Order` class that directly depends on a `Payment` class:

```java
class Order {
    private Payment payment;
```

```java
    public Order() {
        payment = new Payment(); // Concrete dependency
    }

    public void payOrder() {
        payment.pay();
    }
}
```

We can invert the dependency by using an interface:

```java
interface PaymentMethod {
    void pay();
}
```

```java
class Order {

  private PaymentMethod payment;

  public Order(PaymentMethod payment) {
    this.payment = payment; // Abstract dependency
  }

  public void payOrder() {
    payment.pay();
  }
}
```

This way, `Order` depends on an abstraction (`PaymentMethod`) rather than a concrete class.

DRY and KISS

In addition to SOLID principles, two other important design principles in OOP are **DRY** and **KISS**.

Don't Repeat Yourself (DRY)

The **Don't Repeat Yourself** principle states that every piece of knowledge or logic in the system should have a single, unambiguous representation. This principle aims to reduce code duplication, facilitating software maintenance and evolution.

Example:

Suppose we have two methods in a class that perform very similar logic:

```java
class OrderManagement {
    public void
```

```
    sendCustomerNotification(Order order) {
        // Notification sending logic
    }

    public void sendVendorNotification(Order order) {
        // Almost identical notification sending logic
    }
}
```

To adhere to the DRY principle, we can extract the common logic into a separate method:

```java
class OrderManagement {
    private void sendNotification(Order order, String recipient) {
```

```
    // Notification sending logic
}


public void sendCustomerNotification(Order order) {
    sendNotification(order, "customer");
}


public void sendVendorNotification(Order order) {
    sendNotification(order, "vendor");
}
}
```

This way, we reduce code duplication and centralize the notification sending logic.

Keep It Simple, Stupid (KISS)

The **Keep It Simple, Stupid** principle advocates that systems should be as simple as possible and free of unnecessary complexity. This principle encourages simple and elegant solutions that are easier to understand, maintain, and extend.

Example:

Imagine needing to implement a function to calculate the sum of a list of numbers. A complex solution might try to optimize the calculation using complicated algorithms or advanced data structures, but a KISS approach would focus on a simple and direct solution:

```java
int sum(int[] numbers) {
    int total = 0;
    for (int number : numbers) {
```

```
    total += number;
  }
  return total;
}
```

This code is easy to understand and meets the requirements without adding unnecessary complexity.

Design Patterns

Design patterns are recurring solutions to common software design problems. They provide a tried and tested approach to addressing certain design situations, making software more flexible and maintainable.

Characteristics of Design Patterns

Design patterns share some common

characteristics that make them useful tools in software design:

- **Reusability**: Design patterns promote code reusability, as they provide solutions that can be applied to similar problems.

- **Flexibility**: Patterns improve code flexibility, making it more adaptable to future changes.

- **Maintainability**: Using design patterns makes code more understandable and easier to maintain, as patterns are well-documented and known in the developer community.

- **Testability**: Patterns often separate responsibilities and reduce dependencies, making code easier to test.

Examples of Common Design Patterns

There are many design patterns, but some of the most common and useful in OOP include **Singleton**, **Factory**, **Observer**, and **Strategy**.

Singleton

The **Singleton pattern** ensures that a class has only one instance and provides a global point of access to that instance. This is useful in situations where a single object is needed to manage certain resources, such as database connections or a log manager.

Example:

```java
public class LogManager {

    private static LogManager uniqueInstance;

    private LogManager() {
        // Private constructor to prevent external instantiation
    }
```

```java
    public static LogManager getInstance() {
        if (uniqueInstance == null) {
            uniqueInstance = new LogManager();
        }
        return uniqueInstance;
    }

    public void log(String message) {
        System.out.println(message);
    }
}
```

In this example, `LogManager` uses the Singleton pattern to ensure that there is only one instance of this class. The `getInstance` method checks if the instance already exists; if not, it creates it.

Factory

The **Factory pattern** provides an interface for creating objects in a superclass, but allows subclasses to alter the type of object created. This pattern is useful when the creation of an object is complex or depends on conditions that are not known until runtime.

Example:

```java
abstract class VehicleFactory {
    public abstract Vehicle createVehicle();
}

class CarFactory extends VehicleFactory {
    public Vehicle createVehicle() {
        return new Car();
```

```
        }
    }

    class MotorcycleFactory extends VehicleFactory {
        public Vehicle createVehicle() {
            return new Motorcycle();
        }
    }
```

In this example, the `CarFactory` and `MotorcycleFactory` subclasses decide which type of `Vehicle` to create, keeping the creation process abstract in the base class.

Observer

The **Observer pattern** is used when there is a one-to-many relationship between objects, so that when one object changes state, all its dependents are notified and updated automatically. This pattern is commonly used in implementing distributed event-handling systems.

Example:

```java
interface Observer {
    void update(String message);
}


class Subject {
    private List<Observer> observers = new ArrayList<>();
```

```java
    public void attach(Observer observer) {
        observers.add(observer);
    }


    public void notifyObservers(String message) {
        for (Observer observer : observers) {
            observer.update(message);
        }
    }
}
```

In this example, the `Subject` class maintains a list of `Observer` objects that are notified whenever the subject's state changes.

Strategy

The **Strategy pattern** allows an algorithm's behavior to be selected at runtime. This pattern defines a family of algorithms, encapsulates each one, and makes them interchangeable.

Example:

```java
interface PaymentStrategy {
    void pay(int amount);
}

class CreditCardPayment implements PaymentStrategy {
    public void pay(int amount) {
        System.out.println("Paid " + amount + " using Credit Card.");
    }
}
```

```java
class PayPalPayment implements PaymentStrategy {

    public void pay(int amount) {

        System.out.println("Paid " + amount + " using PayPal.");

    }
}


class ShoppingCart {

    private PaymentStrategy paymentStrategy;


    public ShoppingCart(PaymentStrategy paymentStrategy) {

        this.paymentStrategy = paymentStrategy;
    }


    public void checkout(int amount) {

        paymentStrategy.pay(amount);
```

```
        }
    }
```

In this example, the `ShoppingCart` class uses the `PaymentStrategy` interface to allow different payment methods to be chosen at runtime.

Understanding and applying OOP design principles and patterns is essential for building software that is not only functional but also robust, maintainable, and scalable. The **SOLID** principles help ensure that the code adheres to best practices in terms of structure and dependencies, while the **DRY** and **KISS** principles focus on reducing redundancy and complexity. **Design patterns** provide well-established solutions to common problems, making code more flexible and easier to manage. Together, these elements form the foundation of effective object-oriented design, enabling developers to create systems that can evolve gracefully over time.

5. Object-Oriented Programming Languages

Object-Oriented Programming (OOP) has revolutionized the way software is designed and developed, enabling greater modularity, code reusability, and ease of maintenance. Several programming languages have embraced OOP paradigms, each with its own unique features and syntax. In this discussion, we will explore the main OOP languages, such as **Java**, **C++**, **Python**, and **C#**, comparing their characteristics and providing practical examples of OOP usage in each language.

Overview of OOP Languages

Java

Java is one of the most widely used and popular OOP programming languages, developed by Sun Microsystems and first released in 1995. Java was designed to be portable, robust, and secure, with a strong emphasis on object-oriented programming concepts.

Key Features of Java:

- **Platform Independence:** Java is designed to run on any platform that supports the Java Virtual Machine (JVM), making it "Write Once, Run Anywhere" (WORA).

- **Automatic Memory Management:** Java includes a garbage collector that automatically manages memory, preventing many common issues like memory leaks.

- **Rich API:** Java offers a wide range of predefined APIs to handle various aspects of software development, such as user interface management, networking, and database access.

Example of a Class in Java:

```java
```

```java
public class Animal {
    private String name;
    private int age;

    public Animal(String name, int age) {
        this.name = name;
        this.age = age;
    }

    public void makeSound() {
        System.out.println("The animal makes a sound.");
    }

    public String getName() {
        return name;
    }
```

```java
    public void setName(String name) {
        this.name = name;
    }

    public int getAge() {
        return age;
    }

    public void setAge(int age) {
        this.age = age;
    }
}

public class Dog extends Animal {

    public Dog(String name, int age) {
        super(name, age);
    }
```

```
    @Override
    public void makeSound() {
        System.out.println("The dog barks.");
    }
}
```

In this example, `Dog` inherits from the `Animal` class and overrides the `makeSound` method.

C++

C++ is a high-performance programming language developed by Bjarne Stroustrup as an extension of the C language. C++ supports object-oriented programming but also retains support for procedural programming and other paradigms, making it an extremely flexible language.

Key Features of C++:

- **Full Control Over Memory:** C++ gives developers precise control over memory management using pointers and manual memory allocation.

- **Multiple Inheritance:** Unlike many other OOP languages, C++ supports multiple inheritance, allowing a class to inherit from more than one base class.

- **Hybrid Object Model:** C++ allows combining object-oriented programming with procedural programming, making it suitable for applications requiring high performance.

Example of a Class in C++:

```cpp
#include <iostream>
using namespace std;

class Animal {
```

```cpp
protected:
    string name;
    int age;

public:
    Animal(string name, int age) : name(name), age(age) {}

    virtual void makeSound() {
        cout << "The animal makes a sound." << endl;
    }

    string getName() const {
        return name;
    }

    void setName(string name) {
        this->name = name;
```

```cpp
    }

    int getAge() const {
        return age;
    }

    void setAge(int age) {
        this->age = age;
    }
};

class Dog : public Animal {
public:
    Dog(string name, int age) : Animal(name, age) {}

    void makeSound() override {
        cout << "The dog barks." << endl;
```

```
    }
};
```

In this example, the `Dog` class inherits from the `Animal` class and overrides the `makeSound` method, utilizing the concept of polymorphism with virtual methods.

Python

Python is a high-level, interpreted, and dynamic programming language that supports object-oriented programming, alongside many other paradigms such as functional and procedural programming. Python is known for its simplicity and readability, making it popular among both beginners and experienced developers.

Key Features of Python:

- **Simple and Readable Syntax:** Python has a clean and concise syntax, which makes writing and reading code easier.

- **Dynamic Typing:** Python supports dynamic typing, meaning that variable types are determined at runtime, not at compile time.

- **Extensive Libraries:** Python has a vast range of standard and third-party libraries that cover almost any development need, from data processing to machine learning.

Example of a Class in Python:

```python
class Animal:
    def __init__(self, name, age):
        self.name = name
        self.age = age

    def make_sound(self):
```

        print("The animal makes a sound.")

class Dog(Animal):
    def __init__(self, name, age):
        super().__init__(name, age)

    def make_sound(self):
        print("The dog barks.")
```

In this example, the `Dog` class inherits from `Animal` and overrides the `make_sound` method, taking advantage of Python's inheritance and polymorphism.

### C#

**C#** (pronounced "C sharp") is a programming language developed by Microsoft as part of the .NET platform. C# is
```

closely related to Java in terms of syntax and features but also includes many unique functionalities that make it a powerful object-oriented programming language.

Key Features of C#:

- **Integration with .NET:** C# is tightly integrated with the .NET platform, offering native support for resource management, security, and performance optimization.

- **Automatic Memory Management:** Like Java, C# includes a garbage collector that automatically manages memory, simplifying resource management.

- **Support for LINQ and Delegates:** C# introduces advanced concepts such as delegates and Lambda expressions, as well as LINQ (Language Integrated Query) to facilitate data manipulation in a declarative manner.

Example of a Class in C#:

```csharp
using System;

class Animal {
    public string Name { get; set; }
    public int Age { get; set; }

    public Animal(string name, int age) {
        Name = name;
        Age = age;
    }

    public virtual void MakeSound() {
        Console.WriteLine("The animal makes a sound.");
    }
}
```

```
class Dog : Animal {

    public Dog(string name, int age) : base(name, age) {}

    public override void MakeSound() {
        Console.WriteLine("The dog barks.");
    }
}
```

In this example, the `Dog` class inherits from the `Animal` class and uses `override` to redefine the `MakeSound` method, demonstrating the use of polymorphism and properties in C#.

Comparison of OOP Languages

While all these languages support object-oriented programming, there are some significant differences between them that can influence the choice of language for a particular project.

Syntax and Ease of Use

- **Python** is known for its simple and readable syntax, making it ideal for beginners and projects requiring rapid development.

- **Java** and **C#** have more verbose syntax compared to Python but are very similar to each other, with C# offering some advanced features such as delegates and LINQ.

- **C++** is more complex due to its more elaborate syntax and the need for manual memory management, making it more suitable for experienced developers.

6. Applications of OOP

As we have seen, Object-Oriented Programming (OOP) is a programming methodology that organizes software into "objects" representing real-world entities and defines their interactions. This methodology is widely used in various fields of software development. In this discussion, we will explore how OOP is applied in four main areas: software development, web application development, game development, and embedded systems development. We will provide detailed, step-by-step examples for each area, demonstrating the effectiveness and versatility of OOP.

Software Development

Concept

In the context of software development, OOP is used to create modular, scalable, and easily maintainable applications. Objects, classes, inheritance, and polymorphism help structure the code so that it can be easily extended and modified without introducing errors.

Example: Library Management

Consider a library management application that needs to manage books and members. We will use classes to represent books and members and apply inheritance and polymorphism to extend functionalities.

Step 1: Defining Base Classes

We define a `Book` class with attributes and methods to manage the details of a book.

```java
public class Book {
    private String title;
    private String author;
```

```java
    private boolean available;

    public Book(String title, String author) {
        this.title = title;
        this.author = author;
        this.available = true;
    }

    public void reserve() {
        if (available) {
            available = false;
            System.out.println(title + " reserved.");
        } else {
            System.out.println(title + " not available.");
        }
    }
```

```java
    public void returnBook() {
        available = true;
        System.out.println(title + " returned.");
    }

    public String getDetails() {
        return "Title: " + title + ", Author: " + author;
    }
}
```

We create a `Member` class to manage the library members.

```java
public class Member {
    private String name;
    private int id;
```

```java
    public Member(String name, int id) {
        this.name = name;
        this.id = id;
    }

    public String getName() {
        return name;
    }

    public int getId() {
        return id;
    }
}
```

Step 2: Adding Reservation Logic

We create a `Library` class to manage book reservations and returns by members.

```java
import java.util.HashMap;

public class Library {
    private HashMap<String, Book> catalog = new HashMap<>();

    public void addBook(Book book) {
        catalog.put(book.getDetails(), book);
    }

    public void reserveBook(String bookDetails) {
        Book book = catalog.get(bookDetails);
        if (book != null) {
            book.reserve();
```

```
        } else {
            System.out.println("Book not found.");
        }
    }
}
```

Step 3: Using the Classes

We use the created classes to simulate library management.

```java
public class Main {
    public static void main(String[] args) {
        Book book1 = new Book("1984", "George Orwell");
        Book book2 = new Book("The Lord of the Rings", "J.R.R. Tolkien");
```

```
    Library library = new Library();
    library.addBook(book1);
    library.addBook(book2);

    Member member = new Member("Mario Rossi", 1);

        library.reserveBook(book1.getDetails());

library.reserveBook(book1.getDetails()); // Attempt to reserve an already reserved book
    }
}
```

Web Application Development

Concept

In the context of web development, OOP helps organize and manage backend code efficiently. Classes can represent resources, models, and services, while inheritance and polymorphism can be used to extend and customize functionalities.

Example: E-Commerce Site Management

Consider an e-commerce application that manages users and products. We will use classes to represent users and products and implement logic for managing orders.

Step 1: Defining Base Classes

We define a `Product` class to represent the products for sale.

```java
```

```java
public class Product {
    private String name;
    private double price;

    public Product(String name, double price) {
        this.name = name;
        this.price = price;
    }

    public String getName() {
        return name;
    }

    public double getPrice() {
        return price;
    }
}
```

We create a `User` class to represent the site users.

```java
import java.util.ArrayList;
import java.util.List;

public class User {
    private String name;
    private List<Product> cart = new ArrayList<>();

    public User(String name) {
        this.name = name;
    }

    public void addToCart(Product product) {
        cart.add(product);
```

```java
    }

    public void showCart() {
        System.out.println("Cart of " + name + ":");
        for (Product product : cart) {
            System.out.println(product.getName() + " - " + product.getPrice());
        }
    }
}
```

Step 2: Adding Order Logic

We create an `Order` class to manage product purchases by users.

```java
```

```java
public class Order {
    private User user;
    private List<Product> products;

    public Order(User user, List<Product> products) {
        this.user = user;
        this.products = products;
    }

    public void confirmOrder() {
        double total = 0;
        for (Product product : products) {
            total += product.getPrice();
        }
        System.out.println("Order confirmed for " + user.getName() + ". Total: " + total);
    }
}
```

```

#### Step 3: Using the Classes

We simulate the use of classes to manage a cart and an order.

```java
public class Main {
    public static void main(String[] args) {
        Product product1 = new Product("Laptop", 1200.00);
        Product product2 = new Product("Smartphone", 800.00);

        User user = new User("Anna Bianchi");

        user.addToCart(product1);
        user.addToCart(product2);

```
        user.showCart();

        List<Product> orderProducts = new ArrayList<>();
        orderProducts.add(product1);
        orderProducts.add(product2);

        Order order = new Order(user, orderProducts);
        order.confirmOrder();
    }
}
```

Game Development

Concept

In game development, OOP is used to model complex game entities and their interactions. Classes and objects can represent characters, game items, and levels, while inheritance and polymorphism allow for the creation of variants and different behaviors.

Example: Managing Characters and Items in a Game

Consider a simple game that manages characters and items in the game. We will use classes to represent characters and items and implement basic game mechanics.

Step 1: Defining Base Classes

We define a `Character` class to represent game characters.

```java
```

```java
public class Character {
    private String name;
    private int health;

    public Character(String name, int health) {
        this.name = name;
        this.health = health;
    }

    public void attack(Character opponent) {
        System.out.println(name + " attacks " + opponent.name);
        opponent.takeDamage(10); // Fixed damage for simplicity
    }

    public void takeDamage(int damage) {
        health -= damage;
        System.out.println(name + " took " +
```

```java
        damage + " damage. Remaining health: " + health);
    }

    public String getName() {
        return name;
    }
}
```

We create an `Item` class to represent items that characters can collect.

```java
public class Item {
    private String name;
    private String effect;

    public Item(String name, String effect) {
```

```java
        this.name = name;
        this.effect = effect;
    }

    public void use(Character character) {
        System.out.println(character.getName() + " uses " + name + " and " + effect);
    }
}
```

Step 2: Adding Special Characters

We create a `Hero` class that extends `Character` and adds special abilities.

```java
public class Hero extends Character {
    private int specialPower;
```

```java
    public Hero(String name, int health, int specialPower) {
        super(name, health);
        this.specialPower = specialPower;
    }


    public void useSpecialPower(Character opponent) {
        System.out.println(getName() + " uses special power on " + opponent.getName());
        opponent.takeDamage(specialPower);
    }
}
```

Step 3: Using the Classes

We simulate a battle between two characters

and the use of special items.

```java
public class Main {
    public static void main(String[] args) {
        Character warrior = new Character("Warrior", 100);
        Hero mage = new Hero("Mage", 80, 25);

        Item sword = new Item("Magic Sword", "increases attack damage");

        warrior.attack(mage);
        sword.use(mage);
        mage.useSpecialPower(warrior);
    }
}
```

Embedded Systems Development

Concept

In embedded systems development, OOP is used to model and manage the behavior of hardware and software systems that closely interact with the hardware. Classes can represent hardware and software components, managing their interaction in a modular and scalable way.

Example: Managing Sensors and Actuators in an Embedded System

Consider an embedded system for controlling a home automation system that includes sensors and actuators. We will use classes to represent the sensors and actuators and implement the logic to manage their operation.

Step 1: Defining Base Classes

We define a `Sensor` class to represent sensors.

```cpp
#include <iostream>
using namespace std;

class Sensor {
public:
    virtual void readData() = 0; // Pure virtual method
};

class TemperatureSensor : public Sensor {
public:
    void readData() override {
        cout << "Reading temperature
```

```cpp
        data." << endl;
    }
};
```

We create an `Actuator` class to represent actuators.

```cpp
class Actuator {
public:
    virtual void performAction() = 0; // Pure virtual method
};

class LightActuator : public Actuator {
public:
    void performAction() override {
```

```cpp
        cout << "Turning on the light." << endl;
    }
};
```

Step 2: Adding Controller Logic

We create a `Controller` class to manage the sensors and actuators.

```cpp
class Controller {
public:
    void control(Sensor* sensor, Actuator* actuator) {
        sensor->readData();
        actuator->performAction();
    }
};
```

```

#### Step 3: Using the Classes

We simulate the use of the classes to control a sensor and an actuator.

```cpp
int main() {
    TemperatureSensor tempSensor;
    LightActuator light;

    Controller controller;
    controller.control(&tempSensor, &light);

    return 0;
}
```
```

Summary

OOP provides a powerful and flexible approach to software development across different domains. By encapsulating functionality within classes and leveraging inheritance and polymorphism, OOP enables the creation of modular, scalable, and maintainable systems. Whether you are building a library management system, a web application, a game, or an embedded system, OOP offers the tools and techniques needed to manage complexity and facilitate the development process.

7. Testing and Maintenance of OOP Code

Software quality is crucial for the success of any development project. In the context of Object-Oriented Programming (OOP), ensuring that the code is correct, maintainable, and adaptable to changes is essential. In this section, we will explore techniques for testing and maintaining OOP code, including unit and integration testing, maintenance and refactoring practices, and useful tools for testing. We will conclude with some practical exercises to apply these concepts.

Testing Techniques in OOP

Unit Testing

Unit Testing is a technique that focuses on verifying individual units of code, typically methods or classes, to ensure they work correctly in isolation. This type of testing is particularly effective in OOP as it allows for the independent testing of class methods, ensuring each component of the system functions as expected.

Example of Unit Testing in Java

Suppose we have a `Calculator` class with methods for basic arithmetic operations.

```java
public class Calculator {
    public int add(int a, int b) {
        return a + b;
    }

    public int subtract(int a, int b) {
        return a - b;
    }
```

```java
    public int multiply(int a, int b) {
        return a * b;
    }

    public double divide(int a, int b) {
        if (b == 0) throw new IllegalArgumentException("Division by zero");
        return (double) a / b;
    }
}
```

To test this class, we use a testing framework like JUnit in Java.

Calculator Test:

```java
```

```java
import org.junit.jupiter.api.Test;
import static org.junit.jupiter.api.Assertions.*;

public class CalculatorTest {

    @Test
    public void testAdd() {
        Calculator calculator = new Calculator();
        assertEquals(5, calculator.add(2, 3), "Addition should be 5");
    }

    @Test
    public void testSubtract() {
        Calculator calculator = new Calculator();
        assertEquals(1, calculator.subtract(3, 2), "Subtraction should be 1");
    }
```

```java
@Test
public void testMultiply() {
    Calculator calculator = new Calculator();
    assertEquals(6, calculator.multiply(2, 3), "Multiplication should be 6");
}


@Test
public void testDivide() {
    Calculator calculator = new Calculator();
    assertEquals(2.0, calculator.divide(6, 3), "Division should be 2.0");
}


@Test
public void testDivideByZero() {
    Calculator calculator = new Calculator();
    assertThrows(IllegalArgumentException.class
```

```
, () -> calculator.divide(1, 0), "Division by zero should throw an exception");
    }
}
```

Integration Testing

Integration Testing focuses on verifying the interactions between different units of code to ensure they work correctly together. This type of testing is essential in OOP to ensure that classes and their methods collaborate seamlessly.

Example of Integration Testing in Python

Consider an application that manages users and their orders. We have a `User` class and an `Order` class.

User Class:

```python
class User:
    def __init__(self, name):
        self.name = name
        self.orders = []

    def add_order(self, order):
        self.orders.append(order)

    def total_orders(self):
        return sum(order.total() for order in self.orders)
```

Order Class:

```python
class Order:
    def __init__(self, products):
        self.products = products

    def total(self):
        return sum(product.price for product in self.products)
```

Product Class:

```python
class Product:
    def __init__(self, name, price):
        self.name = name
        self.price = price
```

Integration Test:

```python
import unittest

class TestOrderManagement(unittest.TestCase):
    def test_total_orders(self):
        product1 = Product("Laptop", 1200)
        product2 = Product("Smartphone", 800)

        order1 = Order([product1])
        order2 = Order([product2])

        user = User("Anna Bianchi")
        user.add_order(order1)
        user.add_order(order2)
```

```
        self.assertEqual(user.total_orders(), 2000, "The total of orders should be 2000")

if __name__ == '__main__':
    unittest.main()
```

Code Maintenance and Refactoring

Code Maintenance

Code Maintenance involves making changes to existing code to fix bugs, improve performance, or update functionality. In the context of OOP, maintenance can include updating classes, adding new features, and resolving design issues.

**Example: Updating the `Calculator`

Class**

If we want to add a new calculation function to the `Calculator` class, such as square root calculation, we can do it as follows:

```java
public class Calculator {
    public int add(int a, int b) {
        return a + b;
    }

    public int subtract(int a, int b) {
        return a - b;
    }

    public int multiply(int a, int b) {
        return a * b;
    }
```

```java
    public double divide(int a, int b) {
        if (b == 0) throw new IllegalArgumentException("Division by zero");
        return (double) a / b;
    }


    public double squareRoot(double a) {
        if (a < 0) throw new IllegalArgumentException("Number cannot be negative");
        return Math.sqrt(a);
    }
}
```

Code Refactoring

Refactoring is the process of restructuring existing code without changing its external behavior. The goal of refactoring is to improve the code quality, making it more readable, maintainable, and scalable.

Example of Refactoring the `Calculator` Class

Suppose we have repeated methods in the `Calculator` class and want to simplify it:

```java
public class Calculator {
    public int operation(int a, int b, String type) {
        switch(type) {
            case "add":
                return a + b;
            case "subtract":
                return a - b;
            case "multiply":
```

```
            return a * b;
        case "divide":
            if (b == 0) throw new IllegalArgumentException("Division by zero");
            return a / b;
        default:
            throw new IllegalArgumentException("Invalid operation");
    }
  }
}
```

We replaced four separate methods with a single method that handles all operations. This reduces duplication and simplifies maintenance.

Useful Tools for Testing

Tools for Unit Testing

- **JUnit:** A testing framework for Java, widely used for unit testing.

- **NUnit:** A testing framework for .NET, similar to JUnit, for testing C# code.

- **pytest:** A testing framework for Python that supports unit testing and functional testing.

Tools for Integration Testing

- **Postman:** Used to test APIs and web services, useful for integration testing.

- **Mockito:** A mocking framework for Java that facilitates isolated unit testing in complex integration scenarios.

- **TestContainers:** A library for running integration tests with Docker containers, useful for testing applications that depend on external services.

Basic OOP Exercises

Exercise 1: Creating and Testing a `Person` Class

1. **Define the `Person` Class:**

```java
public class Person {
    private String name;
    private int age;

    public Person(String name, int age) {
        this.name = name;
        this.age = age;
    }
```

```java
    public String getName() {
        return name;
    }

    public int getAge() {
        return age;
    }

    public String greet() {
        return "Hello, my name is " + name;
    }
}
```

2. **Test the `Person` Class:**

```java
```

```java
import org.junit.jupiter.api.Test;
import static org.junit.jupiter.api.Assertions.*;

public class PersonTest {
    @Test
    public void testGreet() {
        Person person = new Person("Luca", 25);
        assertEquals("Hello, my name is Luca", person.greet(), "The greeting should be correct");
    }

    @Test
    public void testAge() {
        Person person = new Person("Luca", 25);
        assertEquals(25, person.getAge(), "The age should be 25");
```

        }
    }
    ```

### Exercise 2: Refactoring a `Rectangle` Class

1. **Define the `Rectangle` Class with Errors:**

    ```java
    public class Rectangle {
        private double length;
        private double width;

        public Rectangle(double length, double width) {
            this.length = length;
            this.width = width;

```java
    }

    public double calculateArea() {
        return length * width;
    }

    public double calculatePerimeter() {
        return 2 * (length + width);
    }
}
```

2. **Refactor to Add Validation and Additional Methods:**

```java
public class Rectangle {
    private double length;
```

```java
    private double width;

    public Rectangle(double length, double width) {
        if (length <= 0 || width <= 0) {
            throw new IllegalArgumentException("Length and width must be greater than zero");
        }
        this.length = length;
        this.width = width;
    }

    public double calculateArea() {
        return length * width;
    }

    public double calculatePerimeter() {
        return 2 * (length + width);
```

    }

```
    public double calculateDiagonal() {
        return Math.sqrt(length * length + width * width);
    }
}
```

3. **Test the Refactoring:**

```java
import org.junit.jupiter.api.Test;
import static org.junit.jupiter.api.Assertions.*;

public class RectangleTest {
```

```java
@Test
public void testCalculateArea() {
    Rectangle rectangle = new Rectangle(5, 10);
    assertEquals(50, rectangle.calculateArea(), "The area should be 50");
}


@Test
public void testCalculatePerimeter() {
    Rectangle rectangle = new Rectangle(5, 10);
    assertEquals(30, rectangle.calculatePerimeter(), "The perimeter should be 30");
}


@Test
public void testCalculateDiagonal() {
```

```java
        Rectangle rectangle = new Rectangle(5, 10);
        assertEquals(11.18, rectangle.calculateDiagonal(), 0.01, "The diagonal should be approximately 11.18");
    }


    @Test
    public void testInvalidConstructor() {
        assertThrows(IllegalArgumentException.class, () -> new Rectangle(-5, 10), "Length must be positive");
    }
}
```
```

Testing and maintaining code are fundamental aspects of software development. Using unit and integration testing techniques helps ensure that the code works correctly and that changes do not introduce new bugs. Maintenance and
```

refactoring are crucial for improving code quality and adapting it to changes. Tools like JUnit, Mockito, and pytest are essential for supporting these practices. Practical exercises help apply the discussed concepts and improve skills in managing OOP code.

Index

1. Introduction pg.4

2. Fundamental Concepts of OOP pg.22

3. Fundamental Principles of OOP pg.50

4. Design and Architecture in Object-Oriented Programming (OOP) pg.75

5. Object-Oriented Programming Languages pg.103

6. Applications of OOP pg.118

7. Testing and Maintenance of OOP Code pg.145

www.ingramcontent.com/pod-product-compliance
Lightning Source LLC
Chambersburg PA
CBHW052202220526
45471CB00004B/1774